LOVE & RELATIONSHIPS

AN AQA ESSAY WRITING GUIDE

BY ANTHONY WALKER-COOK
SERIES EDITOR: R. P. DAVIS

First published in 2020 by Accolade Tuition Ltd
71-75 Shelton Street
Covent Garden
London WC2H 9JQ
www.accoladetuition.com
info@accoladetuition.com

ISBN 978-1-9163735-9-4

FIRST EDITION
1 3 5 7 9 10 8 6 4 2

CONTENTS

EDITOR'S FOREWORD

In your GCSE English Literature exam, you will be presented with a single poem from the *Love and Relationships* anthology and a question that invites you to compare and contrast this poem with one other anthology poem of your choosing. Of course, there are many methods one *might* use to tackle this style of question. However, there is one particular technique which, due to its sophistication, most readily allows students to unlock the highest marks: namely, **the thematic method**.

To be clear, this study guide is *not* intended to walk you through the poems line-by-line: there are many great guides out there that do just that. No, this guide, by sifting through a series of mock exam questions, will demonstrate *how* to organise a response thematically and thus write a stellar essay: a skill we believe no other study guide adequately covers!

I have encountered students who have structured their essays all sorts of ways: some by writing about one or both of the poems line-by-line, others by identifying various language techniques and giving each its own paragraph. The method I'm advocating, on the other hand, involves picking out three themes that will allow you to holistically answer the question: these three themes will become the three content paragraphs of your essay, cushioned between a brief introduction and conclusion. Ideally, these themes will follow from one to the next to create a flowing argument. Within each of these thematic paragraphs, you can then ensure you are jumping through the mark scheme's hoops.

So to break things down further, each thematic paragraph will include various point-scoring components. In each paragraph, you will quote from the poem the exam board have set, offer an analysis of these quotes, then discuss how the specific language techniques you have identified illustrate the theme you're discussing. In each paragraph,

A vista of the Yorkshire countryside in Spring. This is perhaps similar to the environs the speaker's friend frequents in Maura Dooley's 'Letters From Yorkshire.'

you will then quote from the second poem (the one you've chosen to write on), and, while analysing these quotes and remarking on language techniques, also explain not only how the second poem relates to the chosen theme, but also how it does so differently (or not!) from the first poem.

Don't worry if this all feels daunting. Throughout this guide Anthony will be illustrating in great detail – by means of examples – how to build an essay of this kind.

The beauty of the thematic approach is that, once you have your themes, you suddenly have a direction and a trajectory, and this makes essay writing a whole lot easier. However, it must also be noted that extracting themes in the first place is something students often find tricky. I have come across many candidates who understand the poems inside out; but when they are presented with a question under exam conditions, and the pressure kicks in, they find it tough to break their response down into themes. The fact of the matter is: the process is a *creative* one and the best themes require a bit of imagination.

In this guide, Anthony shall take nine different exam-style questions, and put together nine essay plans that ensure that every poem in the anthology is discussed in depth at least once. These essay plans will also be accompanied by notes illustrating how we will be satisfying the mark scheme's criteria. Please do keep in mind that, when operating under timed conditions, your plans will necessarily be less detailed than those that appear in this volume.

Swans going about their business. This image may resemble the setting Sheers was imagining in his poem 'Winter Swans.'

Before I hand you over to Anthony, I believe it's worthwhile to run through the three Assessment Objectives the exam board want you to cover in your response – if only to demonstrate how effective the thematic response can be. I would argue that the first Assessment Objective (AO1) – the one that wants candidates to 'read, understand and respond to texts' and which is worth 12 of the total 30 marks up for grabs – will be wholly satisfied by selecting strong themes, then fleshing them out with quotes. Indeed, when it comes to identifying the top-scoring candidates for AO1, the mark scheme explicitly tells examiners to look for a 'critical, exploratory, conceptualised response' that makes 'judicious use of precise references' – the word 'concept' is a synonym of theme, and 'judicious references' simply refers to quotes that appropriately support the theme you've chosen.

The second Assessment Objective (AO2) – which is also responsible for 12 marks – asks students to 'analyse the language, form and structure used by a writer to create meanings and effects, using relevant subject terminology where appropriate.' As noted, you will already be quoting from the poems as you back up your themes, and it is a natural progression to then analyse the language techniques used. In fact, this is far more effective than simply observing language techniques (personification here, alliteration there), because by discussing how the language techniques relates to and shapes the theme, you will also be demonstrating how the writer 'create[s] meanings and effects.'

Now, in my experience, language analysis is the most important element of AO2 – perhaps 8 of the 12 marks will go towards language analysis. You will also notice, however, that AO2 asks students to comment on 'form and structure.' Again, the thematic approach has your back – because though simply shoehorning in a point on form or structure will feel jarring, when you bring these points up while discussing a theme, as a means to further a thematic argument, you will again organically be discussing the way it 'create[s] meanings and effects.'

AO3 requires you to 'show understanding of the relationships between texts and the contexts in which they were written' and is responsible for a more modest 6 marks in total. These are easy enough to weave into a thematic argument; indeed, the theme gives the student a chance to bring up context in a relevant and fitting way. After all, you don't want it to look like you've just shoehorned a contextual factoid into the mix.

Finally, you have AO4 – known also as "spelling and grammar." Technically speaking, there are no AO4 marks up for grabs in this particular section of the paper. That said, I would still suggest that you take care on this front. The examiners are human beings, and if you are demonstrating a strong grasp of spelling and grammar, most examiners (whether rightly or wrongly!) will still be more inclined to mark your paper with greater generosity.

My hope is that this book, by demonstrating how to tease out themes from a pair of poems, will help you feel more confident in doing so yourself. I believe it is also worth mentioning that the themes Anthony has picked out are by no means definitive. Asked the very same question, someone else may pick out different themes, and write an answer that is just as good (if not better– sorry Anthony!). Obviously the exam is not likely to be fun – my memory of them is pretty much the exact opposite.

But still, this is one of the very few chances that you will get at GCSE level to actually be creative. And to my mind at least, that was always more enjoyable – if *enjoyable* is the right word – than simply demonstrating that I had memorised loads of facts.

You'd be surprised how cheaply you can get hold of poetry these days!

Love's Philosophy
By Percy Bysshe Shelley

The fountains mingle with the river
And the rivers with the ocean,
The winds of heaven mix for ever
With a sweet emotion;
Nothing in the world is single;
All things by a law divine
In one spirit meet and mingle.
Why not I with thine?—

See the mountains kiss high heaven
And the waves clasp one another;
No sister-flower would be forgiven
If it disdained its brother;
And the sunlight clasps the earth
And the moonbeams kiss the sea:
What is all this sweet work worth
If thou kiss not me?

Compare the ways poets present romantic love in 'Love's Philosophy' and in one other poem from Love and Relationships.

Introduction

Your introduction should neatly outline your second partner poem, your reasons for choosing it and its connection to the prompt poem. In doing so, you're showing an awareness of both AO3 because you are showing the ways in which texts are connected and AO1 because you're outlining for your examiner the skeleton structure of your 'response'. In the June 2018 Examiner Report, it was noted that candidates that provided an explanation of their second poem with a clear description of the themes to be discussed in the essay produced strong responses.[1]

On this occasion, I have decided to compare Shelley's poem to Owen Sheers' 'Winter Swans'.

"Both 'Winter Swans' and 'Love's Philosophy' focus on nature as a way of expressing ideas about romantic love, but where in the former Sheers depicts a couple who are inspired by nature to begin a relationship, Shelley uses the natural world as a way of convincing a potential lover that they should be together. Nonetheless, to read these poems together means to realise the best and worst of romantic love."

Theme/Paragraph One: Both poets use nature as a frame for their work, but where Sheers uses nature to express genuine emotion, Shelley uses it to convince his partner to sleep with him.

- Indeed the prospect of romantic love for Sheers results in a natural alignment of the world. When the swans of the title surface from the water, Sheers uses a simile to describe them returning 'like boats righting in rough weather', whilst the water around them is described as 'stilling' in the fifth stanza. The poem closes with another simile that notes the closing distance between the speaker and his lover as 'like a pair of wings settling after flight'. Romantic love, ultimately, allows for the world to become calm and uniform. [*AO1 for advancing the argument with a judiciously selected quote; AO2 for the close analysis of the language*]

- That Sheers' poem works towards a 'settling' as described in the final couplet is noted in the poem's structure, which uses six tercets with a closing couplet.[2] This final pairing implies a reconciliation, with the previous three-lined stanzas suggesting the unevenness of their love until then. [*AO2 for discussing how structure shapes meaning*]

- Pivot to comparison: Ironically, Shelley uses a very similar argument in 'Love's Philosophy', but with a very different intention. Shelley's poem partakes in the *carpe diem* topos, imploring the target of the poet's affections to seize the day and kiss him, with other famous examples including Marvell's 'To His Coy Mistress' and Herrick's 'Gather Ye Rosebuds'.[3] As such, Shelley opens the poem with an account of how fountains are connected to rivers, which are in turn connected to the ocean, with an easy enjambment enacting this process of connection. As such, in line five when Shelley states 'Nothing in the world is single', the jarring singularity of the line itself, which is marked at the end by a caesura, emphasises this separation.[4] Shelley's poem thus moves towards completion much like Sheers', but the former poet's intention is less sincere than the latter's. [*AO2 for the close analysis of the language; AO3 for placing the poem in its literary context*]

Theme/Paragraph Two: Both poets also present somewhat idealised depictions of love; however, whereas Shelley's depiction is ultimately self-serving, Sheers' focuses on the latent power of love to meaningfully bring two people together.

- Shelley's title cheekily suggests that the poem has a mantra for love in calling itself a 'philosophy', which implies a theorised and mature approach to love that is at odds with the poem's actual content.[5][*AO1 for advancing the argument with a judiciously selected quote*]
- The Romantic poets, a group that Shelley has retrospectively been assigned to, had a deep appreciation of nature, which supposedly provided them with lessons for life. Yet in 'Love's Philosophy' Shelley, in his desire to show this, almost satirises this tenet of romantic writing, describing how 'the mountains kiss high heaven / And the waves clasp one another'. The natural world can teach us of love, but

only when it suits; this wry tone can be identified at the poem's close, which, having focused on the world around him, resoundingly ends with 'me', implying the true self-serving intention of the speaker's account of nature. [*AO3 for placing the poem in its literary context*]

- <u>Pivot to comparison</u>: Sheers' use of enjambment implies the speaker's desire for love. Connecting stanzas and lines, the reader continues through the poem in the hope of finding answers or a result. Again the swans provocatively represent this desire through Sheers' description of them as 'icebergs of white feather', implying their stability and their unseen power. Focusing on water allows Sheers, in the penultimate stanza, to note how their hands 'somehow' '[swam] the distance between [them]', which gently mirrors his description of how they 'folded, one over the other' at the poem's end. Whereas for Shelly love is self-serving and self-centred, for Sheers it delivers a profound and mutually meaningful union. [*AO1 for advancing the argument with a judiciously selected quote; AO2 for the close analysis of language*]

Theme/Paragraph Three: In Shelley romantic love is over-optimistically presented as positive, but for Sheers there is an awareness of how it can have darker associations.

- Shelley was an atheist, but that does not stop him from using religious imagery throughout 'Love's Philosophy' – such as 'divine', 'one spirit meet and mingle' and 'high heaven' – for effect. This almost saccharine usage, one feels, is an almost hollow attempt to imbue his argument with a sense of divine authorship.[6] [*AO3 for placing the poem in historical context*]

- Pivot to comparison: In 'Winter Swans', the locale in which this conversation takes place is aptly sombre. Observing how the earth is 'gulping for breath' because of too much rain, Sheers suggests the desperation and struggle to find life in such an environment, hence perhaps why the two walk around the lake 'silent and apart'. [*AO1 for advancing the argument with a judiciously selected quote*]

- It is only when the swans come that some optimism is found. Yet, 'Winter Swans' belongs to the poetry collection *Skirrid Hill,* which deals with the themes of disaster and the poet's relationship with his father and the death of his mother.[7] Whilst Sheers' poem can and should be read positively, there are intimations throughout of the dangers romantic love can face. For example, once the speaker's partner notes how swans 'mate for life', the speaker describes them 'like porcelain'. Such an image suggests both the beauty and the fragility of these swans and of love more generally. [*AO2 for the close analysis of language; AO3 for placing the poem in historical context*]

Conclusion

Your conclusion is your last chance to make a lasting impression on your examiner's mind before they give your essay a grade. Try, therefore, to do something different and don't, if possible, begin with 'In conclusion...' Here I ponder on the themes of the poems and the essay more generally.

"Though reading 'Winter Swans' and 'Love's Philosophy' in dialogue implies the latter's depiction of romantic love is merely for show, there is a certain amount of enjoyment that can be found in both. In Sheers, this comes from knowing of the natural correction that comes for the speaker now his relationship can begin, which is something Shelley's speaker can only dream of. Yet, there is an enjoyable cavalier quality to 'Love's Philosophy' that cannot be ignored and maybe Shelley has a point when he asks 'What is all this sweet work worth / If thou kiss not me?' Romantic love is nothing if not playful, after all."[8]

Percy Bysshe Shelley.

Percy Shelley was one of the most influential voices of the Romantic movement.

Porphyria's Lover
By Robert Browning

The rain set early in to-night,
The sullen wind was soon awake,
It tore the elm-tops down for spite,
And did its worst to vex the lake:
I listened with heart fit to break.
When glided in Porphyria; straight
She shut the cold out and the storm,
And kneeled and made the cheerless grate
Blaze up, and all the cottage warm;
Which done, she rose, and from her form
Withdrew the dripping cloak and shawl,
And laid her soiled gloves by, untied
Her hat and let the damp hair fall,
And, last, she sat down by my side
And called me. When no voice replied,
She put my arm about her waist,

And made her smooth white shoulder bare,
And all her yellow hair displaced,
And, stooping, made my cheek lie there,
And spread, o'er all, her yellow hair,
Murmuring how she loved me — she
Too weak, for all her heart's endeavour,
To set its struggling passion free
From pride, and vainer ties dissever,
And give herself to me for ever.
But passion sometimes would prevail,
Nor could to-night's gay feast restrain
A sudden thought of one so pale
For love of her, and all in vain:
So, she was come through wind and rain.
Be sure I looked up at her eyes
Happy and proud; at last I knew
Porphyria worshipped me; surprise
Made my heart swell, and still it grew
While I debated what to do.
That moment she was mine, mine, fair,
Perfectly pure and good: I found
A thing to do, and all her hair
In one long yellow string I wound
Three times her little throat around,
And strangled her. No pain felt she;
I am quite sure she felt no pain.
As a shut bud that holds a bee,
I warily oped her lids: again
Laughed the blue eyes without a stain.
And I untightened next the tress
About her neck; her cheek once more
Blushed bright beneath my burning kiss:
I propped her head up as before,

Only, this time my shoulder bore
Her head, which droops upon it still:
The smiling rosy little head,
So glad it has its utmost will,
That all it scorned at once is fled,
And I, its love, am gained instead!
Porphyria's love: she guessed not how
Her darling one wish would be heard.
And thus we sit together now,
And all night long we have not stirred,
And yet God has not said a word!

Compare the ways poets present desire in 'Porphyria's Lover' and in one other poem from Love and Relationships.

Introduction

Whilst we're encouraging you throughout this book to examine the poems thematically, you must remember that the Love and Relationships anthology spans roughly two-hundred years of writing. This means that some of the poems were written in wildly different times, with different historical and social influences, but others were also written in the same period. In this essay, I'm going to focus on the latter of these situations by examining two poems from the Victorian period (the second being Charlotte Mew's 'The Farmer's Bride').[1] In doing so, from the introduction I'm showing an awareness of historical context and using this to set the two poems in dialogue, thus achieving AO3 from the opening lines!

"Comparing the representation of desire in Browning's 'Porphyria's Lover' and Mew's 'The Farmer's Bride' means to engage with a contemporary debate from the Victorian period: that of the Woman Question. Through this question, the Victorians considered the role of women in society as their political and social powers increased. In spite of this, through the male speakers of their poems, Browning and Mew both show how women were still the focus of intimate desires and how that could easily contain darker tones."

Theme/Paragraph One: Both Browning and Mew use the opening of their poems to establish the nature of and reasons for their speaker's desire, often adopting supernatural or mystical tones.

- Browning emphasises Porphyria's allure from her introduction, using personification and pathetic fallacy to emphasise a petty anger in nature, noting how the wind 'tore the elm-tops down for spite', which is then thrown into relief when Porphyria is said to have 'glided in', a verb that implies an almost-supernatural existence. Porphyria is then juxtaposed with her morose environment, which is created through Browning's use of adjectives: the 'cheerless grate', 'dripping cloak' and 'soiled gloves'. Amidst such a space, desiring Porphyria seems the obvious option. [AO1 for advancing the argument with a judiciously selected quote; AO2 for the close analysis of the language]

- However Browning complicates this later on in the poem by suggesting, in fact, that it was Porphyria who 'worshipped' the speaker. The word 'worship' carries heavy religious undertones, implying this relationship is one of near-fanatical devotion. The domineering confidence of the speaker of Browning's poem enables this shift between the speaker and Porphyria. [*AO1 for advancing the argument with a judiciously selected quote*]

- Pivot to comparison: At the opening of 'The Farmer's Bride', Mew's speaker records: 'Three summers since I chose a maid, / Too young maybe – but more's to do / At harvest-time than bide and woo.' This opening reveals how the speaker has been married for three years, yet in an attempt to deflect any accusations of infertility he notes how sexual relationships are more important than love (or to 'woo'). These lines, in their consideration of whether his bride was 'Too young', to a modern reader may seem uncomfortable, but it was common in the Victorian period for girls to be married in their mid-teens. To then call his bride a 'frightened fay', or a fairy, however, hints towards the rest of the poem's awkward tension between the speaker's desire and his acknowledgement of her near-ethereal hesitancy.[2] [*AO1 for advancing the argument with a judiciously selected quote; AO3 for placing the poem in the historical context*]

Theme/Paragraph Two: The speakers of 'Porphyria's Lover' and 'The Farmer's Bride' are both flawed individuals, which affects our understanding of the nature of their desire.

- 'Porphyria's Lover' is a dramatic monologue, a form that emerged in the 1830s as a reaction to the Romantic period's focus on poetry as the expression of private feeling. The dramatic monologue allows the creation of a character, but in Browning this speaker is an unreliable narrator: we are never fully sure of the nature of his love for Porphyria. [*AO3 for placing the poem in its literary context*]

- Pivot to comparison: Mew's poem is also an example of a dramatic monologue, and again the speaker is a man. Monologues in which bereaved or outcast speakers are able to express their views, with men presented as pitiable and women as physically passionate and strong, is a characteristic of Mew's poetry. This is indicative more widely of the changing attitudes towards women in the Victorian period; for example, in 'The Farmer's Bride', the titular bride is constantly frustrating the wishes of her new groom. Despite being married for three years, the speaker notes how 'I've hardly heard her speak at all.' [*AO3 for placing the poem in its literary and historical context*]

- The structure and language of Mew's poem also emphasises the speaker's irregular thoughts. The various couplet forms throughout 'The Farmer's Bride' ('aabb', 'abab' and 'abba') all imply a speaker who is not learned, which is stressed through Mew's use of irregular vocabulary (for example, 'she runned away'). The rural simplicity that Mew presents, therefore, creates a speaker both coarse and innocent, which both tinge this account of his desire. [*AO2 for the close analysis of the language and for discussing how structure shapes meaning*]

Theme/Paragraph Three: In spite of both speakers declaring their love of their respective women, the use of violence, literal in Browning and threatened in Mew, shows the ways in which women were endangered by male desire.

- The poem's title changed from 'Porphyria' in 1836 to 'Porphyria's Lover' in 1863, which orientates our focus less on Porphyria but on the speaker. This emphasis is seen in the verse form: written in iambic tetrameter, the masculine rhymes imply a male dominance over women.[3] Throughout the poem, then, Browning enables the suggestion of how desire can shift into domination. [*AO2 for discussing how structure shapes meaning; AO3 for placing the poem in its literary context*]

- This shift is also seen in the moment when Porphyria is killed. Wrapping Porphyria's hair around her throat, the speaker turns that which implied her control over him against her. Browning notes how 'Three times' her hair is wrapped around her neck, emphasising such with a delayed triplet ('found', 'wound' and 'around'), with the word separating the first and second of these rhymed words being 'hair'. This surprising moment of violence, matched by the poem's structure, overall stresses the control with which men had over women and the threat women faced daily. [*AO2 for the close analysis of the language*]

- Pivot to comparison: Where Browning depicts the act of murder, Mew implies it throughout her poem through similes that constantly connect the wife to animals. At various points the wife is described as a hare, a mouse and a leveret. These farmyard animals all imply the wife's diminutive flightiness and her weakness. In saying how 'We chased her, flying like a hare', Mew also invites a comparison of the speaker and his wife with the myth of Daphne and Apollo, which focuses on the subjection of women in the name of lust.[4] The implied violence of Mew's poem, then, is as potent as Browning's in showing the dangerous effects desire can have. [*AO1 for advancing the argument with a judiciously selected quote; AO3 for placing the poem in its literary context*]

Conclusion

This conclusion really hones in on the details of Mew's poem, through which I find a connection to Browning. This slight touch shows my detailed knowledge of the poems and suggests a willingness to make connections between them. Note also my continuing AO2 analysis

---

"For all the speaker's frustration in 'The Farmer's Bride', he does not seem to have acted on it: the bride is called a 'maid' in the opening and closing stanza. The groom's longing receives a surprisingly gentle treatment in the final stanza by Mew: 'The soft young down of her, the brown, / The brown of her – her eyes, her hair, her hair!' the speaker recalls. Mew's repetition here might elicit feelings of sympathy from the reader had we not read 'The Farmer's Bride' with Browning's 'Porphyria's Lover', which warns of the dangers for

women presented by their own hair – the male desire
to touch the female body is dangerous."

ESSAY PLAN THREE
'NEUTRAL TONES' & 'LETTERS FROM YORKSHIRE'

Neutral Tones
By Thomas Hardy

We stood by a pond that winter day,
And the sun was white, as though chidden of God,
And a few leaves lay on the starving sod;
– They had fallen from an ash, and were gray.

Your eyes on me were as eyes that rove
Over tedious riddles of years ago;
And some words played between us to and fro
On which lost the more by our love.

The smile on your mouth was the deadest thing
Alive enough to have strength to die;
And a grin of bitterness swept thereby
Like an ominous bird a-wing....

Since then, keen lessons that love deceives,
And wrings with wrong, have shaped to me

Your face, and the God curst sun, and a tree,
And a pond edged with grayish leaves.

Compare the ways poets present distance in 'Neutral Tones' and in one other poem from Love and Relationships.

Introduction

Notice in this introduction the very slight indication of an awareness of how historical contexts shape a poem, priming the examiner for what follows. I've chosen Maura Dooley's 'Letters from Yorkshire', which includes my favourite lines from the entire anthology.

"In Hardy's 'Neutral Tones', there is a distance between the speaker and the person he is with, a former love. The poem's title alone indicates that it is an awkward, loveless meeting. It is a sharp contrast to Dooley's 'Letters from Yorkshire', which presents a teasingly discreet account of the correspondence shared between two people who may or may not be lovers, suggesting how distance is not an insurmountable obstacle for relationships in the modern world."

Theme/Paragraph One: Distance in the two poems has an alternative definition: where Hardy

remembers, Dooley imagines, and this distinction is reflected in the structure of each poem.

- 'Neutral Tones' is made up of four neat quatrains with an 'abba' rhyme scheme, and because of this the poem continuously emphasises separation and togetherness. The 'abba' scheme was the form chosen for Alfred Tennyson's *In Memoriam* (1850), a long poem made of 131 elegiac lyrics; like Tennyson's poem, each line of Hardy's 'Neutral Tones' has the momentum of looking for a pairing.[1] 'Neutral Tones' thus has distance written into its very form, emphasising how Hardy is remembering this episode. [*AO2 for discussing how structure shapes meaning; AO3 for placing the poem in its literary context*]

- Pivot to comparison: Against the formal structure of Hardy's poem, Dooley uses a free verse form.[2] 'Letters from Yorkshire' therefore has a modern, relaxed and conversational idiom that implies a familiarity between the speaker and her addressee. That said, the poem is made of six tercets of equal length, which does suggest the regularity of the correspondence between the two. [*AO2 for discussing how structure shapes meaning*]

- Dooley's speaker states: 'It's not a romance, simply how things are.' Through the caesura and end-stopped line the speaker reveals an unflinching confidence in her situation. Yet Dooley herself has also identified a homesickness in her poem, which is seen in the frequent use of enjambment that stretches across lines and stanzas and that implies a searching for answers that extends throughout the poem. [*AO2 for the close analysis of the language*]

Theme/Paragraph Two: Both poems use nature as a frame to explore ideas of distance. Hardy remembers standing by a pond with his partner in winter and the environment seems to reflect this monotone experience. Dooley, however, juxtaposes her pen-pal's daily routine, which involves working with nature, with her own work that is distant from the natural world.

- Hardy's poem is noticeably without colour, a fact implied by the poem's title, with the opening and closing quatrain emphasising the 'grayish leaves' that have collected around the pond. This monochrome frame implies the circularity of the speaker's thoughts and the sadness that has tinged his experiences. [*AO1 for advancing the argument with a judiciously selected quote; AO2 for discussing how structure shapes meaning*]

- Elsewhere, the poem uses a lexicon of death: the sun is remembered as being 'white, as though chidden of God', which implies the environment itself has been punished, and the mud around the pond is 'starving'.[3] This extends to the speaker's partner: 'The smile on your mouth was the deadest thing / Alive', he remarks. Hardy was 27 when he wrote 'Neutral Tones' and the relationship he describes in the poem never lasted; Hardy's oxymoron thus suggests how the lens through which we view lost love can be distorted. [*AO2 for the close analysis of the language and for discussing how structure shapes meaning; AO3 for placing the poem in historical context*]

- Pivot to comparison: 'Letters from Yorkshire', in

contrast, is decidedly ambiguous about the relationship it describes, but the speaker establishes a clear distinction between her life as a writer and that of her rural correspondent. The immediacy with which the other person, having seen 'the first lapwings return', goes indoors to write to Dooley's speaker however implies a shared fascination with the natural world as his hands attempt to replicate the emergent birdsong ('singing') he can hear. Distance seems not an issue for this couple's correspondence. [*AO1 for advancing the argument with judiciously selected quote*]

Theme/Paragraph Three: Having set up both the definition of distance and establishing the settings of both poems, each poet records different means of communicating with someone in a relationship. Hardy focuses on bodily reactions and Dooley shows what it means to correspond with someone today.

- Hardy's poem describes his partner's face in detail, searching for any clues that might tell him something about their relationship: her eyes look at him 'as eyes that rove / Over tedious riddles', implying both amusement ('rove') and boredom ('tedious') and her aforementioned smile is 'a grin of bitterness'. Yet whatever might be gleaned from this face, Hardy suggests it is not positive: the grin appears 'Like an ominous bird', a portent for their relationship.[4] [*AO1 for advancing the argument with a judiciously selected quote; AO2 for the close analysis of the language*]

- But in the final stanza Hardy implies that he has at least learnt from this experience, and he now thinks of that meeting as part of 'keen lessons' that have taught him that 'love deceives'.
- Pivot to comparison: Dooley's poem reminds us of the role of technology in society today versus that of Hardy's life in the Victorian period. Dooley's speaker is a writer who '[feeds] words onto a blank screen'. Her correspondent might also type (their 'souls tap out messages'), or they may write letters ('into an envelope'). Yet in spite of their geographical distance the two are connected, 'watching the same news in different houses'. [AO3 *for placing the poem in historical context*]

Conclusion

At this point, it's always good to have something new to say – your examiner has already read your essay, so why simply re-write sections of it? It can be a challenge, but one way might be to show what you've learnt from studying these poems, which I've done below.

"At one point in 'Letters from Yorkshire', Dooley asks the rhetorical question 'Is your life more real because you dig and sow?' Though an answer is not forthcoming, Dooley remarks 'it's you / who sends me word of that other world / pouring air and light into an envelope', a beautiful metaphor that emphasises the potential of nature to inspire and rejuvenate. Instead of what Hardy might have us believe, distance might not always be as bad as you would think."

A statue of Thomas Hardy in his home town of Dorchester, UK.

Although 'Walking Away' is about Cecil Day-Lewis parting with his son, Sean, whom Cecil is sending to boarding school, Cecil himself also attended boarding school, and this school (Sherbourne School) is pictured above. We have opted not to reproduce Day-Lewis' poem in full: it is still in copyright and we wish to respect that fact.

Compare the ways in which the parent-child relationship is presented in 'Walking Away' and in one other poem from Love and Relationships.

Introduction

Do be aware of the details behind each poem as they can prove a useful point of connection. Some of the poems studied in this cluster – such as 'When We Two Parted', 'Sonnet 29' and 'Neutral Tones' – were written with specific people in mind. In this essay, I'm going to focus on two other poems that belong to this group – 'Before You Were Mine' (by Carol Ann Duffy) and 'Walking Away' (by Cecil Day-Lewis) – and acknowledging this fact in my introduction means I'm gaining a few AO3 marks early on. Knowing each poem in detail is key, and it will make your own essay planning easier as you'll find various connections.

"Both 'Before You Were Mine' and 'Walking Away' are based on autobiographical events from the poet's lives: in the former, Duffy writes about her mother's life, where in the latter Day-Lewis describes his feelings on the first day his son started at a new school. Both poems are about one individual in the parent-child relationship trying to understand the other, and the difficulties that come with that."

Theme/Paragraph One: Through the opening and structure of both poems, Duffy and Day-Lewis emphasise the theme of separation.

- From the opening of 'Walking Away' Day-Lewis shows how the changes that are coming will be permanent, for although the seasons are changing (summer into autumn, as implied by the observation how the 'leaves [are] just turning') the playing field lines are 'new-ruled', which implies the forging of fresh divisions, specifically the divide between father and son. [*AO1 for advancing the argument with judiciously selected quotes*]

- This new balance is registered in the poem's rhyme scheme of 'abaca', which allows both union in the first, third and fifth line of each quintet, and change in the second and fourth. Separation thus punctuates the poem and inflects its depiction of the parent-child relationships. [*AO2 for discussing how structure shapes meaning*]

- Pivot to comparison: 'Before You Were Mine' likewise uses markers of distance to register a gap between the speaker and her mother: the openings of the first three stanzas mark how the two are apart, such as 'I'm not here yet' and the focus on the ten years before the poet was born, which are thought to have been the 'best'. Each quintet of the poem is devoted to a separate memory, and thus the structure of the poem also emphasises how the speaker is looking back into her mother's life and her own to facilitate this meditation on motherhood. [*AO2 for discussing how structure shapes meaning*]

Theme/Paragraph Two: Both poems are inspired by real events, but there are qualities in both that also make them applicable to all parents and children.

- 'Walking Away' was inspired, according to Sean Day-Lewis, the poet's son, by his first day at school in 1938. Writing in 2018 to the *Guardian,* Sean said 'it is a memory poem' that is 'addressed to all caring parents at all times'. Certainly, details in the poem support the claim that it refers to an autobiographical event, such as the opening observation that is 'eighteen years' since the events described occurred. Children achieving independence is shown to be a universal event through the poem's use of bird imagery ('half-fledged' and 'eddying away') and a biblical reference at the poem's close: 'God alone' refers to Jesus' sacrifice. The physical end of parent-child relationships is thus proven to have a continuing impact on the adult, with Day-Lewis going so far as to suggest that it 'Gnaws at my mind still', an uncomfortable image. [*AO1 for advancing the argument with judiciously selected quotes; AO3 for placing the poem in historical context*]

- Pivot to comparison: Duffy also balances the specific with the universal in 'Before You Were Mine'. In the first stanza, the references to Maggie McGeeney and Jean Duff with her mother, who are all laughing ('shriek'), and her billowing dress invites the speaker to compare her to 'Marilyn.' Duffy refers to Marilyn Monroe, a Hollywood sex symbol of the 1950s who represented glamour and tragedy. Monroe tragically died aged 32 of a drug overdose following a battle with addiction. Duffy stresses throughout the poem her mother's changed life once her child was born, hence perhaps Marilyn is an apt figure as an expression of both joy and future sadness. [*AO3 for placing the poem in historical context*]

- In the third stanza, Duffy states she sees the projected memory of her mother as 'clear as scent', which is both a simile and oxymoron.[1] These shoes that prompt this comment evocatively capture the mother's essence, to which is added the final note about the 'small bites on your neck, sweetheart?' in which the parent-child relationship is reversed. [*AO1 for advancing the argument with a judiciously selected quote; AO2 for the close analysis of language*]

Theme/Paragraph Three: As these poets explore their parent-child relationships, their priority – as hinted at through the universal imagery already discussed – appears to be communicating in ways that readers find relatable.

- Day-Lewis juxtaposes two similes in 'Walking Away' to imply his coming to terms with the situation presented to him. The first – 'like a satellite / Wrenched from its orbit' – is unnatural in its focus on the grandiose and esoteric.[2] However, by the third stanza it seems as if Day-Lewis is beginning to come to terms with the event, for the second simile – 'Like a winged seed loosened from its parent stem' – is much gentler in tone. Comparing the verbs in each simile, 'Wrenched' with 'loosened', shows this shift in attitude. [*AO2 for the close analysis of the*

*language and for discussing how structure shapes
meaning*]

- Pivot to comparison: Against these similes might be
  compared Duffy's use of her own memories with her
  mother: 'I remember my hands in those high-heeled
  red shoes,' she recalls, 'relics, / and now your ghost
  clatters towards me over George Square'. Calling
  these shoes 'relics' imbues them with an almost-
  religious status. Duffy's focus on touch in the quote is
  also juxtaposed with the image of the mother's 'ghost',
  with the repeated 'h' and 'r' sounds adding a light
  clattering to the lines as if re-capturing something of
  what it once was to hear those shoes be walked in.
  [*AO1 for advancing the argument with a judiciously
  selected quote; AO2 for the close analysis of language*]

- Though 'Before You Were Mine' was written in 1993,
  it is set in the 1950s. This context provides an
  interesting frame for the theme of motherhood as it
  allows Duffy to note how it has changed over the past
  fifty years. Duffy's grandmother ('Ma'), for example,
  waits for her daughter to come home late from a dance
  to give out a 'hiding', which is broadly indicative of
  changing attitudes towards physically punishing
  children (mature or not). There is also a note of
  unrestricted freedom in Duffy recording in the final
  quatrain that her mother taught her the cha cha 'on
  the way home from Mass'. These small details imply
  the increasingly lax attitudes towards parenting and
  religion during the twentieth century, but even then
  the daughter wishes for 'the bold girl winking in
  Portobello'. [*AO3 for placing the poem in historical
  context*]

Conclusion

A neat way to conclude your essay can be to focus on the final lines of each poem. This way, you'll still be scoring AO1 or AO2 marks depending on how you do it; this method allows you to reflect on the themes of both the question and brings your essay to a natural close.

"To write of the parent-child relationship means to write of one of the most primal of bonds. Both poets write of the past, but where Day-Lewis writes of his son, Duffy writes of her mother, and both end with distinctively different tones. Day-Lewis focuses on religion and the lesson that 'selfhood begins with a walking away, / And love is proved in the letting go.' In Duffy, however, the mother figure with whom she has connected pre-dates her own existence: she is imbued with a 'glamorous love' that she had 'before you were mine.' For a parent trying to understand a child, or visa versa, the principle challenge, it seems, is to first let go."

A sari, as picture above, is a type of traditional Indian garb. In Nagra's 'Singh Song', the speaker's wife wears a tartan sari: an non-traditional take on a traditional item of clothing. We have opted not to reproduce 'Singh Song' or Simon Armitage's 'Mother Any Distance' in full: both are still in copyright and we wish to respect that fact.

Compare the ways in which independence is presented in 'Mother, any distance' and in one other poem from Love and Relationships.

Introduction

The more imaginative you can be in correctly identifying themes for each poem, the more flexible you will be in your exam. For example, in this essay on independence I'm going to examine Daljit Nagra's 'Singh Song', which, although it is predominantly about romantic love, has a focus on the speaker growing apart from his parents. The more thinking about the poems you do before the exam, the higher chance you'll have of opening the exam paper and feeling confident about the essay ahead of you.

"Armitage's 'Mother, any distance' offers a general account of a child moving into their first home, with independence barely achieved. Nagra's 'Singh Song', however, presents a newly married Indian couple and their integration both within the groom's family and in English culture. Both poems, despite these differences, ultimately reveal how difficult it can be to achieve independence."

Theme/Paragraph One: Both poems are about a desire for independence, but their speakers betray an immaturity through their poetic voice.

- Though Armitage's poem depicts a scene of a person's increasing maturity, there are hints throughout the work that imply he is still slightly immature: for example, describing the 'acres of the walls, the prairies of the floors', whilst aptly capturing the enormity of the situation, is in its hyperbole not dissimilar to the way in which a child conceptualises space.[1] *[AO1 for advancing the argument with a judiciously selected quote; AO2 for the close analysis of language]*
- Elsewhere, Armitage suggests he 'space-walk[s] through the empty bedrooms', not only emphasising a child-like imagination but also how he feels weightless or hollow at the opportunity ahead. Thus even though the speaker is about to become independent, there is the intimation that he still has a way of viewing the world that belongs to a child. *[AO1 for advancing the argument with a judiciously selected quote]*
- <u>Pivot to comparison:</u> A similar tension can be detected throughout Nagra's 'Singh Song', the speaker of which runs 'just one' of his 'daddy's shops'. This slight detail overall suggests the speaker's diminutive status, which is emphasised by his unfocused attitude towards work: aside from closing the shop to have sex (or to make 'luv'), when he does return it is with his 'pinnie untied' and he then faces an angry set of customers who accuse him of having 'di worst Indian shop / on di whole Indian road'. *[AO1 for advancing the argument with judiciously selected quotes]*

Theme/Paragraph Two: Armitage uses the form of the poem to pose his own growing independence as a question to the reader, and Nagra likewise plays with our expectations, subtly inviting the reader to ask whether his independence from his parents can counterbalance his emerging dependence on his bride.

- 'Mother, any distance' belongs to a poetry collection called *Book of Matches*, a series of sonnets written about the brevity of everyday life and that are supposed to be read in the amount of time it takes for a match to burn. Sonnets were traditionally used in legal disputes as the form allows logical arguments to be presented; but does 'Mother, any distance' solve a problem? In the final stanza the speaker goes to the top of the house and imagines how 'two floors below your fingertips still pinch / the last one-hundredth of an inch...' Armitage's ellipsis is full of the potential that awaits him in his independence, but the notion of his mother impossibly holding on to a 'one-hundredth of an inch' also conveys a desperation.[2] It is uncertain, then, quite how the speaker feels about this defining separation. [AO3 *for placing the poem in its literary context*]

- Pivot to comparison: Nagra also engages with the reader's expectations through 'Singh Song', but this is noted in the poem's title, which plays on the notion of 'sing song', a designation for basic poetry, and 'Singh', a word that all Sikh men take as part of their names and that means lion. With the poem's mock phonetic Punjabi accent and comic lines Nagra therefore challenges the boundaries of English love poetry to reflect other cultural experiences of growing up in Britain. [*AO3 for placing the poem in its literary-historical context*]

- For all his wife's remissible actions, the speaker is clearly infatuated with her still, always returning to 'my bride' as the poem goes on. The relationship is evidently new – he calls her 'bride', not 'wife' – and as part of this he is still learning about her, hence why he describes her as having 'tiny eyes ov a gun / and di tummy ov a teddy'. Nagra's metaphors juxtapose her danger with a plump cuteness, suggesting the heady intoxication of this different love poem. Thus whereas Armitage's speaker poses his independence as an open question, Nagra's poem coyly avoids any easy sense of resolution as the speaker navigates his growing independence from his parents and the imaginative freedoms that come with this. [*AO2 for close analysis of the language*]

Theme/Paragraph Three:Both poems use slight details to emphasise the increasing gap – physical in Armitage and cultural in Nagra – between the children and their parents.

- At the beginning of the second stanza, Armitage's speaker notes 'You at the zero-end, me with the spool of tape', an appropriate metaphor for how a child begins with their mother but then, as the years go on and the numbers in the reel increase, a distance grows between them. [*AO2 for the close analysis of the language*]
- In the description of the measuring of the house in the

second stanza, Armitage uses enjambment to literally enact the 'recording / length' happening around him. Stretching across lines laden with caesuras just as the tape measure is being twisted around the shell of the house's walls, the poem captures the reeling uncertainty that comes with this momentous occasion. Appropriately, Armitage ends the stanza by juxtaposing two objects: 'Anchor. Kite.' The implication is that the speaker will either sink or fly, two apt metaphors for coming of age. [AO2 *for the close analysis of the language and for discussing how structure shapes meaning*]

- Pivot to comparison: Nagra, whose parents were shopkeepers, uses 'Singh Song' to emphasise the experience of immigrants in Britain. The poem jovially plays to Indian stereotypes but also captures the changes occurring between first- and second-generation immigrants. For example, the speaker's wife is said to 'hav a red crew cut / and she wear a Tartan sari', she mocks the speaker's father and swears at his mother and she glamorously wears high heels (stanza four), all of which emphasise her integration within Western culture – the younger generation of 'Singh Song' achieve independence in part by creating their own hybrid personality. [AO3 *for placing the poem in its historical context*]

Conclusion

"Both 'Mother, any distance' and 'Singh Song' show how independence takes time: children do not automatically become adults. Yet the endings of both poems are also filled with hope: Nagra revels in the speaker's joy of his 'priceless' love and Armitage's speaker is presented with 'an endless sky / to fall or fly.' Independence, it seems, is inevitable, but it is also exciting."

A farmer operating a two horse plough: similar to the plough Seamus Heaney's father uses in 'Follower.' We have opted not to reproduce Heaney's poem in full: it is still in copyright and we wish to respect that fact.

Compare the ways in which memories are presented in 'Follower' and in one other poem from Love and Relationships.

Introduction

"Seamus Heaney's 'Follower' writes of a man looking back on his childhood and his father, whom he adores and idolises. Against the actuality of Heaney's memory might be contrasted Charles Causley's 'Eden Rock', an ambiguous reminiscence that sets heart-felt emotion within an uncanny environment. Real or not, however, both poems are indicative of the role of the imagination in remembering our parents and how that shapes our memories of them."

Theme/Paragraph One: Heaney and Causley use distinctive settings in their poems to depict their memories.

- Heaney dashes technical language referring to farming throughout 'Follower' to emphasise to the reader both the setting and his father's skill. Yet at the same time these words are intimately connected with Heaney's memory. That he 'stumbled in his hobnailed wake', for example, refers both to the father's boots, which had nails hammered into the bottom for extra grip, and to his father's power and situation. [*AO1 for advancing the argument with a judiciously selected quote; AO3 for invoking relevant historical context]*

- <u>Pivot to comparison:</u> Against Heaney's real setting, Causley's 'Eden Rock' sets his engagement with his parents in a liminal space.[1] Causley said of the locale of 'Eden Rock' that he had 'no idea' of where the place was and that he 'made it up'. Yet the word 'Eden' reverberates with biblical overtones, referring back to Adam and Eve and their paradise. Added to this is the age of Causley's parents – the father is twenty-five and the mother twenty-three, creating them as almost immortally young figures and making their meeting with a supposedly mature Causley almost impossible. [*AO3 for placing the poem in its historical context*]

- Added to this is the poem's consistent use of half rhymes – for example 'dress' and 'grass' in stanza two – that imbues the poem with an unnatural feel throughout so that, as we read of this meeting, we are aware that something is not quite as it should be. [*AO2 for the close analysis of language*]

Theme/Paragraph Two: Essential to Heaney's memory is the description of his father working the land as a farmer. Causley, by contrast, imagines an idealised version of his parents.

- Throughout *Death of a Naturalist,* the poetic collection in which 'Follower' was published, Heaney engages with the ways in which the art of poetry and the craft of rural work can be connected. Though the verse form structure of Heaney's poem – a steady iambic tetrameter – emphasises the regularity of the

father's work, the rhyme scheme – which is roughly
'abab' with the 'a's' often half rhymes – is
demonstrative of the rural setting and environment.[2]
This is, as suggested by the technical language, a
world of labour, not perhaps of poetry. [*AO2 for
discussing how form shapes meaning; AO3 for placing
the poem in its literary context*]

- Heaney's memories of his father working are tinged
  with the naïve admiration a son has for his father. For
  example, in the opening stanza he remembers how
  'His shoulders globed like a full sail strung / Between
  the shafts and the furrow'. Heaney's simile impresses
  his father's size, and the term 'globed' has a joyful
  hyperbole to it. [*AO2 for the close analysis of
  language*]

- Pivot to comparison: Where Heaney obviously knew
  his father, Causley's died of injuries sustained during
  World War One. Causley also had to care for his
  mother before she died in 1971 ('Eden Rock' was
  written in 1988). The simile 'The sky whitens as if lie
  by three suns' creates a glaringly bright locale in
  which Causley's ever-young parents shine with a
  youthful amour, pouring milk 'From an old H. P.
  Sauce bottle' and skipping stones across the water.
  [*AO3 for placing the poem in historical context*]

**Theme/Paragraph Three: Ultimately, both poets
depict their parents within a sentimental frame,
but both also emphasise a sense of irrevocable
transition at the end of their poems, adding a
sadness to these memories.**

- Causley emphasises his separation from his parents by breaking the final quatrain into two uneven sections. The first three lines have his parents 'beckon to me from the other bank' and encourage him to cross the water in-front of him, but to offset this idyll the poem concludes 'I had not thought that it would be like this.'[3] At the end of 'Eden Rock', it is unclear exactly what situation Causley has described, but in this final point of separation he emphasises his solitary life and confusion. [*AO1 for advancing the argument with a judiciously selected quote; AO2 for discussing how structure shapes meaning*]

- <u>Pivot to comparison:</u> In the second stanza, Heaney refers to his father simply as 'An expert.' Heaney's use of a caesura reveals the confidence and adoration he had for his father's ability. The intimate descriptions of his father's work are however tragically deflated in the final stanza where the tense changes in the final lines from past to present tense and Heaney records 'But today / It is my father who keeps stumbling / Behind me, and will not go away.' Because of the poem's insistence of the skill and ability of Heaney's father, there's an intense sadness in this closing description that recognises how nature reverses and, whereas children mature, adults revert back to an infantile state, a theme famously described by the melancholy Jacques in Shakespeare's *As You Like It*. [*AO2 for discussing how structure shapes meaning; AO3 for placing the poem in its literary context*]

Conclusion

It can be nice to conclude your essay by bringing in a relevant poem that is not from the anthology so long as it is thematically relevant; that way, you'll continue to accrue AO3 marks and it'll give you something fresh to say, which isn't always easy at the end of an essay. Here I'm using a second poem by Heaney to comment on the theme of the essay (memory, in case you've forgotten). Note also my light digging pun in the final sentence – anything to make your work stand out to an examiner!

"It was previously noted that throughout *Death of a Naturalist* Heaney balances his desire to write with his rural background. This distinction is made in another of his poems, 'Digging', which again focuses on Heaney's father. The poem concludes 'Between my finger and my thumb / The squat pen rests. / I'll dig with it.' The two poems analysed depict memories tinged with idealism, yet in carefully reading these works we realise how the relationship between children and their parents refuses to be buried under the recesses of time."

ESSAY PLAN SEVEN
'SINGH SONG' & 'BEFORE YOU WERE MINE'

Seward Johnson's statue of Marilyn Monroe, recreating her pose from the film *The Seven Year Itch*. It is this pose Carol Ann Duffy invokes in 'Before You Were Mine.' We have opted not to reproduce Duffy's poem in full: it is still in copyright and we wish to respect that fact.

Compare the ways in which admiration is presented in 'Before You Were Mine' and in one other poem from Love and Relationships.

Introduction

For this plan I'm revisiting 'Singh Song' and 'Before You Were Mine', in which the person being admired is different. Other, more obvious, poetic choices for this topic might include 'Follower' and 'Climbing My Grandfather', but I'd always encourage you to think widely about the poems in your revision and essay planning.

"The speakers of 'Singh Song' and 'Before You Were Mine' admire someone: in the former it is a new bride, whereas in the latter it is her mother. Across these poems, in looking at the ways in which the poets introduce the admired, note generational differences, and express private moments, it becomes apparent how love tinges those whom we adore or aspire to learn about."

Theme/Paragraph One: In their introductions of the admired, Nagra and Duffy depict both good and bad qualities of the admired person, but this tells us something of the relationship shared between them and the speaker.

- At the beginning of 'Singh Song' the speaker reveals how he runs 'just one ov my daddy's shops', which suggests he has yet to be given a lot of responsibility. This is, however, probably a good thing, as he often locks the shop if it is empty and goes to his 'newly bride'. The excitement of this relationship is suggested in the word 'bride': the marriage is still new. The two then make 'luv' and 'share' food. This introduction to the wifethus reveals both the speaker's happiness at his marriage and her power over him. These quotes also are indicative of the mock Punjabi accent throughout 'Singh Song', which Nagra uses to imitate the voices of those who have immigrated to Britain and the consequent mix of cultures. [*AO1 for advancing the argument with a judiciously selected quote; AO3 for invoking relevant historical context*]

- Yet this novel marriage is also indicated in how the husband defines his wife: 'tiny eyes ov a gun / and di tummy ov a teddy'. This juxtaposition of dangerous eyes with other adorable bodily features is indicative of how the two do not yet fully understand one another but in its simplicity there emerges an adoring tone from the speaker to his wife. Alongside this is an immaturity towards sex: the speaker calls it a 'tickle'. Though he admires his wife, he defines her in these child-like terms. [*AO2 for the close analysis of the language*]

- Pivot to comparison: Where 'Singh Song' depicts a sexual relationship, Duffy's poem describes a mother-daughter relationship. Where Nagra's bride is living and breathing, Duffy's focus comes from a photograph and the past. Three of the poem's four quintets open with declarations of distance – for example, 'I'm ten years away from the corner you laugh on'. In the picture, Duffy sees two women ('Maggie McGreeny and Jean Duff') next to her mother, whose 'polka-dot dress blows round your legs,' which evokes the famous image of 'Marilyn' Monroe in the film *The Seven Year Itch*. Monroe represented not only Hollywood glamour but also the potential for a tragic fate (she died aged 32). Duffy's reference thus establishes her mother's beauty and prepares readers for the darker understanding of her future that comes in the poem's later stanzas. [*AO2 for discussing how structure shapes meaning; AO3 for placing the poem in its historical context*]

- The structure of 'Before You Were Mine' stresses the focus on memory in the poem, which sets the focus on Duffy's admiration for her mother. Each quintet depicts a memory and the contemporary blank verse allows for a free, unrestricted recall of those qualities and events that led to such adoration.[1] [*AO2 for discussing how structure shapes meaning*]

Theme/Paragraph Two: Both poems present generational differences that reveal how the admired person fits within their contemporary context.

- When the wife is introduced in 'Singh Song', she is given a position of power: 'Above my head high heel tap di ground / as my wife on di web is playing wid di mouse'. It seems his wife runs her own internet business ('her Sikh lover site'), and through this introduction Nagra emphasises her strength and power. The wife's rapping pushes out the voices of the customers, and from there the speaker always returns to 'my bride', an admiring refrain that punctuates the poem. [*AO1 for advancing the argument with a judiciously selected quote*]

- 'Singh Song' captures the experiences of second-generation immigrants living in Britain, and the wife in the poem represents how various cultures influence an individual. For example, she has 'a red crew cut' and a 'Tartan sari'. She also does not seem to respect the older generation ('she effing at my mum') and the speaker joins her in 'making fun at my daddy'. [*AO3 for placing the poem in historical context*]

- Pivot to comparison: Duffy asks in the third stanza 'The decade ahead of my loud possessive yell was the best one, eh?' This conversational rhetorical question introduces the idea that Duffy's birth took her mother away from her actual desires, yet the next image – 'I remember my hands in those high-heeled red shoes, relics,' – combines the two. Duffy's repeated 'h' and 'r' sounds enact this tapping, yet the contemplative caesura also suggests how she is aware of the future, with the word 'relic' imbuing these objects with an almost-religious power. [*AO1 for advancing the argument with a judiciously selected quote; AO2 for the close analysis of the language*]

Theme/Paragraph Three: The speakers in both poems yearn to learn more about the individuals they admire. In Duffy's poem, the speaker wants to explore her mother's past, whereas Nagra's speaker takes joy in the brief interludes during which he is permitted to bond with his wife.

- As 'my bride' is a refrain throughout 'Singh Song', Duffy often returns to the idea of what it meant for the mother to live 'before you were mine'. In the second stanza, which depicts her mother at a dance, this theme is expressed through the heady description of the event, 'the fizzy, movie tomorrows' with the note on how her mother ('your Ma') was ready to give 'a hiding' for coming home late, reminding us today how physical punishment was a typical aspect of parenting in the mid twentieth century. [*AO3 for invoking relevant historical context*]

- The final stanza of 'Before You Were Mine' concludes the exploration of how a child can desire to learn of a parent before they were born. Even when remembering learning how to dance (a supposedly joyful memory) Duffy 'wanted the bold girl winking in Portobello'. Duffy's use of enjambment throughout the poems leads to this sense of searching in an intimate attempt to learn more about her mother.

- <u>Pivot to comparison:</u> Despite how cavalier the speaker's wife is presented, in the final stanzas of the poem Nagra shifts to a surprisingly touching description of how the two share their aspirations. The two sit in the closed shop behind 'chocolate bars' and look outside. The short conversation recorded has the speaker conclude that his wife is 'priceless', a tender conclusion to the depiction of a relationship that has otherwise seemed about sex and immaturity. [*AO1 for advancing the argument with a judiciously selected quote*]

Conclusion

Both poems have the admired person wearing high heels – I'm going to focus on this detail for my conclusion to summarise the themes of my essay (and it allows for a nice pun).

"These contemporary poems depict different types of admiration: where Nagra explores the naive lust of a young, newly-married couple, Duffy's poem powerfully shows a child's quest to learn more about their parent in an attempt to understand them. A vital object in both poems is a pair of high heels, which represent power and glamour; walking in another's footsteps is not always an easy task."

Sonnet 29
By Elizabeth Barrett Browning

I think of thee!—my thoughts do twine and bud
About thee, as wild vines, about a tree,
Put out broad leaves, and soon there 's nought to see
Except the straggling green which hides the wood.
Yet, O my palm-tree, be it understood
I will not have my thoughts instead of thee
Who art dearer, better! Rather, instantly
Renew thy presence; as a strong tree should,
Rustle thy boughs and set thy trunk all bare,
And let these bands of greenery which insphere thee
Drop heavily down,—burst, shattered, everywhere!
Because, in this deep joy to see and hear thee
And breathe within thy shadow a new air,
I do not think of thee—I am too near thee.

Compare the ways poets use nature to talk about relationships in 'Sonnet 29' and in one other poem from Love and Relationships.

Introduction

For this particular essay, I have decided to invoke Andrew Waterhouse's 'Climbing my Grandfather'.

"The types of relationships presented in 'Sonnet 29' and 'Climbing my Grandfather' are different: the former expresses romantic love whereas the latter is more of an admiration for a family member. Yet in both poems nature is key to the expression of these relationships – comparing the two means to acknowledge how strength and danger is innate in nature, and, perhaps, in relationships too."[1]

Theme/Paragraph One: Nature allows for an expression of love that is tinged with darkness and danger.

- The opening lines of 'Sonnet 29' outline how the speaker thinks about her love when they are apart: 'I think of thee! – my thoughts do twine and bud / About thee as wild vines, about a tree, / Put out broad leaves, and soon there's nought to see.' Several elements of this opening that emphasise nature's controlling power warrant attention: firstly, the use of enjambment enacts the twining described; secondly, the use of internal rhyme ('thee' and 'tree', which is then matched with 'see' in the next line) adds to the sense of enrapture; finally, the use of the word 'broad' implies the extensive control of these thoughts. The opening of the poem thus shows how nature has the potential to be controlling. [*AO1 for advancing the argument with a judiciously selected quote; AO2 for the close analysis of the language*]

- Pivot to comparison: From the opening of 'Climbing my Grandfather', 'I decide to do it free, without a rope or new.', Waterhouse establishes the tension that exists between the unharnessed freedom of growing up and the dangers that come with this independence. Firmly located in the present tense, there is a pregnant excitement in this opening, as nature can be wondrous and terrifying. In spite of this, there is a respect for nature throughout 'Climbing my Grandfather' that is reminiscent of the romantic poets, who were often poetically inspired by the awe-inducing power of mountains.[2] [*AO1 for advancing the argument with a judiciously selected quote; AO3 for placing the poem in its literary context*]

Theme/ Paragraph Two: The structure of both poems is an essential aspect of how both poets write about nature in relation to their respective relationships.

- Waterhouse uses an extended metaphor throughout

'Climbing my Grandfather': that is, he imagines himself as a climber trying to surmount his grandfather, which is an expression of the speaker's attempts to get to know this older member of the family. As he explains in the fourth line, he is 'trying to get a grip.' Waterhouse creates this effect by integrating mountaineering language – 'overhanging', 'purchase' and 'screed' – throughout the poem alongside the steady description of the grandfather. These words also emphasise the challenge of learning about someone else. [AO2 *for the close analysis of the language*]

- These difficulties are also represented in the structure of the poem. Waterhouse's free verse form creates the suggestion of an untamed, craggy mountain to be surpassed. Through the lack of a rhythm and free use of enjambment, however, Waterhouse also implies a relative ease to this challenge in making the poem flow easily. [AO2 *for discussing how structure shapes meaning*]

- Pivot to comparison: Barrett Browning uses the sonnet form to express her concerns about the relationship. Sonnets, split into an octave and a sestet, traditionally pose a question and an answer. The shift between the two usually occurs at line nine and is called a volta, yet in 'Sonnet 29' Barrett Browning begins this switch in line 7 with the imperative 'instantly / Renew thy presence; as a strong tree should, / Rustle thy boughs and set thy trunk all bare'. This structural shift with the strong poetic voice bolstered by the imperatives implies both how the twining emotions have perhaps confused the speaker but also the forceful power of her desires.³ [AO2 *for the close analysis of the*

language; AO3 for placing the poem in its literary
context]

Theme/Paragraph Three: Amidst nature, however, both Waterhouse and Barrett Browning manage to reveal true emotion, with the environment acting as a conduit for the poets to present emotions in a simple yet beautiful way.

- 'Sonnet 29' was written when Elizabeth was courting Robert Browning, who would become her husband. As such the poem is thought to be about Browning. The focus on nature in 'Sonnet 29' allows Barrett Browning to express her love. That she calls the addressee 'a strong tree' is indicative of how she perceives him – sturdy and reliable – but she also calls him 'my palm-tree'. Palms have biblical connotations, specifically Jesus' triumphant return to Jerusalem. Barrett Browning was religiously inclined, and so this label attaches to her lover a sense of power and a tone of victory to their love, which is appropriate given the poem's movement towards clarity and understanding. [*AO3 for placing the poem in literary and historical context*]
- Pivot to comparison: Waterhouse was an environmental campaigner, and hence the extended metaphor is particularly apt as it allows for a natural tone of respect towards both the grandfather and nature to emerge throughout the poem. In the final line Waterhouse shifts from the intensely physical description of ascent to one of moving simplicity where, having reached the summit, he lies back and

describes 'feeling his [grandfather's] heat, knowing / the slow pulse of his good heart.' Whilst the idea of a 'good heart' is almost naïve, this simplicity allows for a gentle conclusion to the poem that again emphasises how nature can be an apt lens through which to write of relationships. [*AO1 for advancing the argument with a judiciously selected quote; AO3 for placing the poem in historical context*]

- Despite the speaker's attempt at maturity in 'Climbing my Grandfather', there are hints throughout the poem of the speaker's immaturity. One example is the simile 'the skin of his finger is smooth and thick / like warm ice.' Waterhouse's simple oxymoron contrasts the repeated emphasis throughout the poem on the grandfather's age, such as his 'old brogues', the 'old stiches' of a scar and the 'earth-stained hand.' [*AO1 for advancing the argument with a judiciously selected quote*]

Conclusion

Another way of concluding your essay is to bring in another poem from the collection. So long as you use this poem to succinctly reflect on the themes you have discussed, this neat little way of tying up your work will provide a fresh perspective and will show your knowledge of the collection further.

"As noted at the opening of this essay, the relationships depicted in 'Sonnet 29' and 'Climbing my Grandfather' are of different natures. It is apt, then, to conclude with a quote from Dooley's 'Letters from Yorkshire', in which the speaker describes how their friend '[pours] air and light into an envelope' when the two write to each other. Expressing relationships through the frame of nature allows for the intangibility of love to be expressed even if, as Waterhouse and Barrett Browning realise, it is not always an easy or positive experience.

A portrait of Elizabeth Barrett Browning. She married Robert Browning, the author of 'Porphyria's Lover.'

When We Two Parted
By George Gordon Byron

When we two parted
In silence and tears,
Half broken-hearted
To sever for years,
Pale grew thy cheek and cold,
Colder thy kiss;
Truly that hour foretold
Sorrow to this.

The dew of the morning
Sunk chill on my brow –
It felt like the warning
Of what I feel now.
Thy vows are all broken,
And light is thy fame;
I hear thy name spoken,
And share in its shame.

They name thee before me,
A knell in mine ear;
A shudder comes o'er me—
Why wert thou so dear?
They know not I knew thee,
Who knew thee too well—
Long, long shall I rue thee,
Too deeply to tell.

In secret we met—
In silence I grieve,
That thy heart could forget,
Thy spirit deceive.
If I should meet thee
After long years,
How should I greet thee?—
With silence and tears.

Compare the ways in which loss is presented in 'When We Two Parted' and in one other poem from Love and Relationships.

Introduction

For this final essay I'm returning to 'Walking Away' because the nature of loss described in the poem is of a different kind to that in Byron's poem, thus creating an interesting comparison that invites a thematic focus. Note also throughout my analysis of 'Walking Away' how I'm focusing on some of the same poetic techniques but suggesting an alternative reading of them: herein lies the skill of AO2, which is showing how an author makes meaning and backing that up with textual examples.

"For all of Byron's boisterous personality and history, 'When We Two Parted' seems a genuine account of the sadness at losing a loved one. Though very different in situation, Day-Lewis' 'Walking Away' likewise is filled with emotion. Alongside these compositional differences, there are comparisons to be made with how both poems conceive of loss and reputation and the role of emotion in presenting such."

Theme/Paragraph One: Both poets conceive of loss in different ways: Byron uses a rhetoric of death, whilst the changing similes in Day-Lewis' poem implies how the speaker is coming to terms with his son growing up.

- The rhetoric of death that is dotted throughout 'When We Two Parted' both conveys Byron's disappointment at the end of the affair and implies that perhaps the relationship was already over. For the former interpretation, readers should note the use of the word 'knell' that is used to describe how the speaker feels when he hears his lover's name or the suggestion that 'In silence I grieve'; for the latter, in the first stanza he describes how 'Pale grew thy cheek and cold, / Colder thy kiss', suggesting his lover is like a corpse. These words and phrases create a melancholic tone throughout the poem that expresses the speaker's overall sadness at the situation. [*AO1 for advancing the argument with a judiciously selected quote*]

- Alongside this is a strong awareness through the poem of the speaker's now-unrequited love of the addressee.[1]'Long, long shall I rue thee,' he states, 'Too deeply to tell', with the repetition of 'long' imbuing the lines with regret and sorrow. Hence perhaps the ambiguity in the earlier suggestion in the first stanza that the two were 'Half broken-hearted': it was only the speaker who was sorry to see the relationship end.

- Pivot to comparison: 'Walking Away' is about Sean, Day-Lewis' son from his first marriage to Mary King that eventually ended in 1951. Day-Lewis' similes throughout 'Walking Away' register his loss. In the first, the son is 'like a satellite / Wrenched from its orbit', which implies the violence of the situation. 'Walking Away' was written in 1956 but is based on Sean's first day at school in 1938 – 'satellite' here refers not to the technological meaning of the word (Sputnik was launched in 1957) but a natural object caught in the pull of an orbit.[2]In the second simile, however, Day-Lewis acknowledges a much more gentle image – 'Like a winged seed loosened from its parent stem' – that suggests he is coming to terms with his son growing up and that such a break is not so cataclysmic for the natural progression of life. [*AO2 for the close analysis of the language; AO3 for placing the poem in historical context*]

Theme/Paragraph Two: Focusing on the presentation of reputation realises how both poems

conceive of loss as an experience shared by society.

- 'When We Two Parted' is thought to have been written about Lady Frances Webster, with whom Byron had a secret affair. The poet even went so far as to suggest that he wrote the poem in 1808 to protect Webster's identity. It was actually written in 1816. Small details throughout the poem suggest the damaging effect that having an affair could have on a woman's reputation (or her 'fame'), which is now thought to have become 'light', whilst the man seems to have escaped such repudiation ('They know not I knew thee'). That said, Byron was known for many scandalous relationships with both men and women during his life. [AO3 *for placing the poem in historical context*]

- The speaker also notes how 'I hear thy name spoken, / And share in its shame', with the alliterative 'sh' sound almost capturing the whispered nature of these utterances. The word 'name' is then repeated in the third stanza: the speaker's loss is thus amplified by society, which implies the incessant threats posed to a woman who engaged in affairs. [AO2 *for the close analysis of the language;* AO3 *for invoking relevant historical context*]

- Pivot to comparison: Though much of 'Walking Away' is specific to Day-Lewis and his son, Sean – for example the specificity in the opening note of 'It is eighteen years ago, almost to the day' – Sean has commented recently that 'It is a memory poem' and one that all parents can appreciate and relate with. The bird imagery throughout 'Walking Away' adds to this: the son is like 'a half-fledged thing set free' who is slowly 'eddying away'. Caught now in the winds of time, the son moves away from his father with a sadness ('pathos') because he is un-prepared: he 'finds no paths where the path should be.'

Theme/Paragraph Three: The structure of both poems emphasises the emotion behind their composition.

- At the poem's close Byron repeats the word 'silence and tears', but where the first instance implies how both participants in the relationship acknowledge the sadness of its ending ('When we two parted / In silence and tears'), the second is focused solely on the speaker. Should the speaker see his ex-lover after so many years (and, presumably, having heard of her exploits from others), he would now greet her 'With silence and tears'. Byron's repetition, whilst it acknowledges some acceptance on his part, does show how long-lasting the effects of a relationship can be even for a man of Byron's reputation. [*AO2 for the close analysis of the language and for discussing how structure shapes meaning*]
- Byron's 'ababcdcd' rhyme scheme lends an emphasis to the end of each couplet; in spite of their separation these words find a pair, an act that the speaker can no longer achieve with his desired beloved. [*AO2 for discussing how structure shapes meaning*]
- Pivot to comparison: Day-Lewis uses an 'abaca' scheme throughout the quintets of 'Walking Away', which means separation and change is emphasised throughout the poem with only a hint of potential

harmony in the first, third and fifth lines. Sean attended a boarding school, which enforced a separation between parent and child, and Cecil also boarded when he was younger – 'Walking Away' thus registers an alternative aspect (that of the parent) to the traditional English tradition of sending children to boarding school. [*AO2 for discussing how structure shapes meaning; AO3 for placing the poem in historical context*]

- The final quintet of 'Walking Away' opens with the observation 'I have had worse partings, but none that so / Gnaws at my mind still.' The animalistic 'Gnaws' shows how the primal link between father and son is here being disrupted. [*AO2 for the close analysis of the language*]

Conclusion

"Both poems acknowledge how losing a loved one is a challenging and emotional experience. Yet both also suggest that it is a cathartic experience from which an individual can emerge both stronger and enlightened.[3] Byron asks in his poem 'Why wert thou so dear?' and at the end of 'Walking Away' Day-Lewis concludes with the suggestion 'selfhood begins with a walking away': loss thus need not always be conceived of negatively, for it can teach even as its hurts."

A bust of Lord Byron.

NOTES

ESSAY PLAN ONE

1. Do make sure that part of your revision (for any exam) is reading as many Examiner's Reports as are available on the exam board's website: they often provide a wealth of tips about what students did well and, perhaps even more importantly, where they went wrong!

2. Just to remind you: 'stanza' is the name we give to verses generally; a 'couplet' refers to a two-line stanza, a 'tercet' to a three-line stanza, a 'quatrain' to a four-line stanza, a 'quintet' to a five-line stanza, and a 'sestet' to a six-line stanza.

3. Cavalier poetry was a popular seventeenth-century movement that focused on joyful and simple lyrics. Central to their poetry was a mentality of *carpe diem*, which is Latin for 'seize the day.'
   A topos is basically a literary topic.

4. Caesura is when a poet inserts punctuation midway through a line of poetry, thereby creating a pause.

5. Don't forget that titles, as with the poems themselves, are generally constructs and can be commented on. Be aware, however, that some titles are just the first line of the poem, for example Armitage's 'Mother, any distance.'

6. If something is saccharine, it means it is overly sweet.

7. Do spend a little bit of time researching the poetry collections from which the individual poems you study come from – they can tell you a lot about the overarching themes and the poet themselves.

8. The use of 'cavalier quality' here is a pun on the *carpe diem* motif; for using puns in the conclusion, see Essay Plan Six.

ESSAY PLAN TWO

1. The Victorian period is roughly said to have occurred during the reign of Queen Victoria, which spanned from 1837 until 1901.

2. A fay is a fairy.

3. A masculine rhyme is a rhyme in which the rhymed word is stressed; a feminine rhyme would have the word unstressed.

4. The myth of Daphne and Apollo is told in Ovid's *Metamorphoses*. The god Apollo chases after the young nymph Daphne in blind lust. The young

girl's only way of escaping is to be turned into a laurel tree. The story is often thought to represent a battle between chastity and sexual desire.

ESSAY PLAN THREE

1. An elegiac poem is a mournful poem used to commemorate the dead.
2. Free verse poetry is poetry that does not rhyme and that does not have a regular rhythm.
3. The *Oxford English Dictionary* defines 'lexicon' as 'The vocabulary proper to some department of knowledge or sphere of activity; the vocabulary of word-stock of a region, a particular speaker, etc.' Basically, it's a scheme of reference.
4. A portent is a sign or omen that something bad is going to happen; think The Grim in *Harry Potter*!

ESSAY PLAN FOUR

1. An oxymoron is a phrase that combines two contradictory ideas. A famous one is spoken by Shakespeare's Romeo: 'O loving hate!' The ideas of love and hate are contradictory, hence this is an oxymoron.
2. Something grandiose is something that seems impressive and imposing – so much so that it almost seems pretentious.

   If something is esoteric, it means it is obscure and requires expert knowledge to fully understand.

ESSAY PLAN FIVE

1. Hyperbole is very similar in meaning to the word exaggeration.
2. An ellipsis is when you have three full stops in a row.

ESSAY PLAN SIX

1. 'Liminal' means to be at the boundaries of something, but it also has undertones of the uncanny or supernatural.
2. You may well also be asking: what does 'iambic tetrameter' mean? Let me start from the top.

   GCSE students have often heard of the phrase 'iambic pentameter' when learning about Shakespeare. The first word – iamb – refers to something called a metrical foot, whereas the word 'pentameter' refers to the fact that almost all of Shakespeare's lines have five metrical feet per line.

It is almost certainly easiest to illustrate this with an example. Let's take the second line from Shakespeare's *Romeo and Juliet*; however, we are going to mark out each metrical foot with a vertical line, and all of the stressed syllables with bold font: 'In **fair** | Ve**ro**| na, **where** | we **lay** | our **scene.**' As you can see, each metrical foot here is made up of two consecutive syllables, making five metrical feet in all – hence pentameter. You can also see that the stress in each metrical foot is on the second syllable. This is what makes the metrical foot an iamb.

Now, in Heaney's poem, we do not have an iambic *pentameter*; we have an iambic *tetrameter*. The word *tetrameter* simply means that, instead of five iambs per line, you have four. So let's look at a line from 'Follower' and mark out the syllables and feet in the same way as we did with the line from Shakespeare: 'I **stum** | bled **in**| his **hob** | nailed **wake.**' As you can see, we have four consecutive iambs, hence tetrameter.

If you have three iambs per line, you have an iambic trimester. And two would be an iambic dimeter.

3. An 'idyll' is a peaceful and calm location, and often associated with the pastoral genre.

ESSAY PLAN SEVEN

1. Blank verse is when you have poetry written in iambic pentameter and that does not rhyme. A large amount of the verse in Shakespeare's plays are written in blank verse.

ESSAY PLAN EIGHT

1. If something is innate it is inborn or natural.
2. For those of you willing to make the ascent and do some extra reading, you can learn more about the romantics and mountains by reading Coleridge's 'Hymn before Sun-rise in the Vale of Chamouny', Shelley's 'Mont Blanc: Lines Written in the Vale of Chamouni', and Wordsworth's 'View from the Top of Black Comb'. A little closer to the Love and Relationships cluster, you could also read Day Lewis' 'Transitional Poem'.
3. An imperative is an order.

ESSAY PLAN NINE

1. Unrequited love is a love that is not returned.
2. The Space Race was a vital part of the Cold War that began with the launching of Sputnik in 1957. From then on, U.S. and Soviet competed to scientifically conquer space, the next frontier.

3. Catharsis is a process of emotional relief that is often associated with art and literature. Aristotle wrote especially of how catharsis is an essential part of consuming the arts.

ACCOLADE PRESS FOR GCSE
ENGLISH: THE RANGE

www.accoladetuition.com/accolade-gcse-guides

ENGLISH LITERATURE

Romeo and Juliet: Essay Writing Guide for GCSE (9-1)

Macbeth: Essay Writing Guide for GCSE (9-1)

Power and Conflict: Essay Writing Guide for GCSE (9-1)

Dr Jekyll and Mr Hyde: Essay Writing Guide for GCSE (9-1)

A Christmas Carol: Essay Writing Guide for GCSE (9-1)

The Merchant of Venice: Essay Writing Guide for GCSE (9-1)

Unseen Poetry: Essay Writing Guide for GCSE (9-1)

Great Expectations: Essay Writing Guide for GCSE (9-1)

An Inspector Calls: Essay Writing Guide for GCSE (9-1)

Pride and Prejudice: Essay Writing Guide for GCSE (9-1)

The Tempest: Essay Writing Guide for GCSE (9-1)

Lord of the Flies: Essay Writing Guide for GCSE (9-1)

Much Ado About Nothing: Essay Writing Guide for GCSE (9-1)

ENGLISH LANGUAGE

English Language Paper One: A Technique Guide for GCSE (9-1)

English Language Paper Two : A Technique Guide for GCSE (9-1)

If you found this book useful, please consider leaving a review on Amazon, which you can do at the following link: **https://rcl.ink/6RwbT**

You can also join our private Facebook group (where our authors share resources and guidance) by visiting the following link: **https://rcl.ink/DME.**

Printed in Great Britain
by Amazon